TURN
AROUND
TIME

DAVID GUTERSON

TURN
AROUND
TIME

A WALKING POEM FOR THE PACIFIC NORTHWEST

ILLUSTRATIONS BY JUSTIN GIBBENS

MOUNTAINEERS
BOOKS

TO ALL MY HIKING PARTNERS,

PAST AND PRESENT

MOUNTAINEERS BOOKS is dedicated to the exploration, preservation, and enjoyment of outdoor and wilderness areas.

1001 SW Klickitat Way, Suite 201, Seattle, WA 98134
800-553-4453, www.mountaineersbooks.org

Printed in Canada
Distributed in the United Kingdom by Cordee, www.cordee.co.uk
22 21 20 19   1 2 3 4 5

Copyeditor: Janice Lee
Design and layout: Jen Grable
Illustrations: Justin Gibbens

Library of Congress Cataloging-in-Publication Data
Names: Guterson, David, author.
Title: Turn around time : a walking poem for the Pacific Northwest / David
   Guterson.
Other titles: Walking poem for the Pacific Northwest
Description: Seattle, WA : Mountaineers Books [Leicester] : Distributed in the
   United Kingdom by Cordee 2019.
Identifiers: LCCN 2019000478 | ISBN 9781680512656 (hardcover)
Subjects: LCSH: Northwest, Pacific—Poetry. | Mountaineering—Poetry. |
   Mountains—Poetry. | LCGFT: Narrative poetry.
Classification: LCC PS3557.U846 T87 2019 | DDC 811/.54—dc23
LC record available at https://lccn.loc.gov/2019000478

Printed on FSC-certified materials

ISBN (hardcover): 978-1-68051-265-6

An independent nonprofit publisher since 1960

ACKNOWLEDGMENTS

Friends Richard Kenney and Michael Drake were invaluable early readers of *Turn Around Time*. My editor at Mountaineers Books, Kate Rogers, has made the poem much better than it would have been if left solely to me. Jen Grable, senior designer and production manager at the press, is largely responsible for the great beauty and refinement of the physical object you hold in your hands. Janet Kimball, managing editor at Mountaineers Books, has been an enthusiastic advocate for *Turn Around Time* every step of the way. In short—no author publishes in a vacuum. Every book comes into the world because of many hearts and minds. I have been blessed by good fortune during this collaboration. It has been a pleasure every step of the way.

I need a separate paragraph for artist and illustrator Justin Gibbens, who is extraordinarily gifted, amiable to a fault, diligent, selfless, and inspiring. Justin is a native Washingtonian with a long outdoor track record, a lover of forests, mountains, and rivers, and possessed, simultaneously, of the humility and confidence that makes collaboration productive and a pleasure. Thank you, Justin, for illustrating this book, and for your goodwill and friendship on our journey together.

Turn Around Time is meant to be rhythmically propulsive, to the point that footnotes would do it a disservice; yet such notes are needed if I'm to give credit where credit is due.

To begin at the beginning, then: the quoted material on page 27 was derived from the "Routes Report" section of the Cascade Climbers website. That we're "here as on a darkling plain" on page 44 derives from Matthew Arnold's (over-anthologized) poem "Dover Beach." The "old stone savage" on page 53 is borrowed from Robert Frost's poem "Mending Wall." The "poontang" on page 58 lies between quotation marks to reinforce that the use of the term is the responsibility of a woodland trail-troll berserker devil-bear and not condoned or sanctioned by the poet. The opening line of section 12 of "Out" owes a debt to Hemingway's *Big Two-Hearted River*.

"The world's flaming and shaking today, counter, original, spare, strange," on page 76 borrows explicitly from Gerard Manley Hopkins's poem "Pied Beauty." The "lover's quarrel with the world" on page 78 is a direct lift from Frost's poem "A Lesson for Today" (the words also grace his gravestone). "Tatters in our dress" on page 80 is an approximation of the phrase "every tatter in our mortal dress" found in William Butler Yeats' poem "Sailing to Byzantium." The "narrow road to the interior" on page 90 is borrowed from Matsuo Bashō. The long quote on page 105 is from Virginia Woolf's 1927 essay "Street Haunting: A London Adventure." Philip Larkin's lament on page 107 is from his poem "Aubade." The quoted material on page 134 is from John Milton's *Paradise Lost*. The poem's final stanza is largely indebted to the Ten Ox Herding pictures of Zen Buddhism.

—*David Guterson*

INTRODUCTION

My uncle Henry Shain was a member of The Mountaineers and an avid, energetic hiker and climber. Standard when I was young was for Henry and his outdoor associates to converge in North Bend at Twede's Cafe, eat breakfast off the griddle, then carpool to one trailhead or another, where they laced up boots saturated with Ome Daiber's miracle concoction sold under the trade name Sno-Seal. Henry knew Daiber personally, not because he moved in an atmosphere of high-profile alpinists, but because Seattle, in the mid-twentieth century, had a tight-knit hiking and climbing community. When I tagged along on Mountaineers trips, a lot of hikers looked familiar.

Henry was enthusiastic but not sentimental or romantic in his view of the natural world. He hadn't read Wordsworth, Thoreau, or Muir, but he had read substantially in academic geology, in local history, and in guides to flora. He liked mountaineering lore. His mind held fast to facts and numbers. He knew the dates and circumstances of Mount Rainier climbing disasters. Six foot four, lanky but broad-shouldered, Henry literally dragged me up Mount Dickerman when I was small. On his advice, I held on to his pack while he made a direct ascent in snow, and in this way we summited. Later I walked coming-of-age trails in the Central Cascades with Henry. We made off-trail forays in the

Alpine Lakes Wilderness before it was the Alpine Lakes Wilderness. Years later we traversed the Bailey Range together. At that point, Henry was seventy-six and spent a lot of time bent over with his pack facing the sky and his hands on his knees, halted and working to slow down his breathing. He didn't want to quit. It all meant too much to him. He lies now beneath a tombstone inscribed with the words "He loved the mountains."

From the playground behind my junior high school in Seattle I could see, on a clear day, both the Olympics and the Cascades. I felt drawn toward both ranges but couldn't get to either often enough. Then someone told me that Boy Scout Troop 173 overnighted once a month year-round, and I joined. The troop was divided, in military fashion, into "patrols" of a few boys each, so it was fellow patrol members I tented and camped with. My patrol leader at one point was named Don Harder. You can Google "Don Harder climber" if you want details, but suffice it to say that when I knew Don, he was already an experienced and skilled technical rock climber. Don goaded and derided me with amicable fervor. He was in the Scouts for no other reason than to hike and camp, and so was I. We also had in common a mutual friend, Marc Emerson, who'd died on Castle Rock near Leavenworth, Washington, at sixteen. Marc's father had been part of the '63 Everest expedition, which was composed significantly of Western Washingtonians. I had no idea at the time what a local heyday it was, and was anyway innocent of high alpine ambition and of interest in rock walls. I just wanted to roam, and did, with other people who also desired the freedom of the hills.

The day after taking my last high school final, I got a ride from my sister to Randle, Washington, where I went to work for the US Forest Service on a brush-disposal crew. The clear-cutting of timber was then reaching a zenith. Logging trucks barreled out of the mountains recklessly, the mills ran three shifts, glowing at night, and choker setters took home eight dollars an hour, or three times what I was paid. A lot of Randlelites were flush enough to eat at Tall Timber or at the Mount Adams Cafe, or to drive up to Centralia to buy gear at Yard Birds. Randle was unincorporated and nebulous. It had no center other than Fischer's Market, a grocery store not far from the bridge across the Cowlitz River. We summer USFS employees bought food and sundries there, refrigerated our cases of beer in a stream, and slept in a bunkhouse. The guy bunking to my left began each day by starting up a turntable and playing Led Zeppelin's *Houses of the Holy*—always side two, which began with "Dancing Days." Most guys rose then, but some refused to stir for another quarter hour, having closed down the Big Bottom Tavern the night before, and having staggered in darkness up Silverbrook Road to drink more in the bunkhouse. No matter. By seven forty-five, all were on the clock. Sometimes we piled brush in partial cuts, but mostly we ran fire suppression against sizable slash burns. These blazes were usually initiated at dusk, when fuel moisture felt prime and the wind had died down. If all went well, we stood around and watched a monstrous conflagration, but far too often a bad burning strategy meant flames jumped the line, leaving us to scramble in smoke-filled woods—and in a welter of wee-hour shouting and confusion—to lay out a new fire line and hold it.

I spent four summers in Randle, which meant proximity to Rainier, the Goat Rocks, Mount Adams, and Mount St. Helens, and daily dwelling in the high country. At the end of my third season I climbed Adams via the northwest ridge, overnighting on its summit; at the end of my fourth I walked the Pacific Crest Trail through the Goat Rocks. After that I got a job teaching English at Olympic College and another teaching composition in the Navy College Program for Afloat College Education on the base in Bremerton. These work circumstances oriented me toward the Olympic Mountains, about which I became both studious and romantic; I wanted to go up every river valley there, and over every pass. Henry had bequeathed me his worn USGS topographic quadrangle maps, to which, in this era, I took a magnifying glass in search of passable off-trail contours. I had what I thought was an advantage in this arena, because Henry had introduced me to Robert L. Wood, whose *Olympic Mountains Trail Guide* (along with *Climber's Guide to the Olympic Mountains*, later retitled *Olympic Mountains: A Climbing Guide*) was sine qua non for Olympics obsessives. At times I besieged Wood with my off-trail imaginings, about which he was unequivocally negative. Wood would stay silent while I went on at length, letting me say what I had to say in full, at which point he would answer "No, it can't be done" before launching his own, more sober soliloquy, one composed of multiple perils and replete with impassable cliff faces or miles of old-growth tree fall.

Wood was correct in tone and spirit. My friends and I had no idea what we were doing. Years afterward I looked at maps and read route descriptions with a view toward determining just how idiotic we'd now and then been. Sure enough, we'd had no business fooling around on Mount Garfield freestyle or scaling certain cliffs on Mount Anderson without protection. More often, though, we were restless and kept moving, as if there was indeed a destination—increasingly off-trail, increasingly in new terrain—crossing multiple and far-flung ranges on longish and overloaded expeditions. As it turned out, elk knew better than we did about paths of least resistance between drainages, and were also better guides than maps were.

The first-person narrator of my novel *The Other* says something I ought to say at this juncture, with a view toward putting things in current context: "Since those days, I've become a trail hiker, someone who takes no chances in the woods but goes to them frequently, in all weathers." I remain avid, willing, ready, and even eager, but am more than content now to tread familiar trails, where the beauty of change is forever in evidence—ribbons of backwater reorienting from year to year, the scouring of cutbanks proceeding by inches, new rockfall, fresh avalanche scars. I don't see these things as mere consolations. They aren't hued in the gold tint of passing years. The beauty of change is as thrilling to me now as new terrain was thrilling to me then. I'm post–turn around time, and so I have turned back to walk among previously unnoted mysteries.

Wood's *Olympic Mountains Trail Guide*; Fred Beckey's three-volume *Cascade Alpine Guide*; Ira Spring, Bob Spring, and Harvey Manning's many hiking volumes; and Olympic Mountain Rescue's *Climber's Guide to the Olympic Mountains*—these mid- to late twentieth-century books (all published by Mountaineers Books) once formed a library of local urtexts for climbers and foot travelers in the mountains of Western Washington. Each had navigational efficacy, and each had local, eccentric charms. The Spring brothers and Manning, always celebratory and lighthearted, traded in faux crankiness and affectionate complaints (crowds, mosquitoes, I-90, development); Beckey rigorously erased himself so as not to subvert attentiveness to nuance (no climber could blame him for a misconstrued pitch); Wood was conscientious and scrupulous to a fault, prone to nostalgia, stylistically lush; and the collectively written *Climber's Guide to the Olympic Mountains*—a compilation of summary route descriptions—incorporated in its pages rough art and terse syntax. All these books were good backcountry companions and could be browsed at home, too, as goads to new places (or as reprimands for past bad judgment, or as indulgences in memory). They were fingers pointing at the moon.

Turn Around Time: A Walking Poem for the Pacific Northwest has no place in this down-to-earth pantheon. It's a trail guide at best only figuratively, and only if one conceives of life as a journey. I hope it avoids a guide's perilous presumptions—that it speaks to just one way among the myriad, that it admits to ambiguity and is willing to get lost. That it moves toward the unknown. That it tends toward a reach forever out of reach. That it leads readers into a world both familiar and strange—familiar as a kind of inchoate inner language, strange in its conjunctions and perplexing visitations. I've refused herein to intimate clarity where none indeed exists, for fear of leading readers to a cul-de-sac.

"Turn around time" is an alpinist's notion—that preplanned moment when, no matter what, it's time to reverse course and head back. The principle acknowledges an unstoppable coming darkness and the prospect of tragic outcomes spurred by hubris; it mitigates against both; it commits to the prudent; it speaks against enticement; it wells up in the pit of the stomach when a summit makes its siren's call. All this to say that it's fundamentally rational. Many narratives of fatality compel it. There's no small irony in the fact that turn around time gets established—or not— long before it's needed. Our fate is laid down far in advance. Already, now, we're dictating our futures. It can be too late very early, as it turns out.

For every route, in every season, in all weathers—according not to our lights but to our condition in sum—there is indeed a time to turn around. On the standard route at the summer solstice, lofted by a fortunate breeze, even then this bell tolls, and if we haven't committed in advance of duress, fooling ourselves and those around us instead, if we can't take our elevation, can't believe in preemption, prefer our own rules for a game we didn't invent, well then, we will look twice and then thrice at our digital clocks and make the first of those accommodations that, in accretion, seals all. The biggest risk is, and always has been, us, by nature and volition both. Maybe bows to complaisance, made early, do their work. Maybe deepening denial, or willful ignorance, scores us. We knew at base camp, over tea, in sunlight, that turn around time was ahead of us, but—a lump of sugar, please.

It's easier to turn around if, in view of the summit, you see that no summit actually exists. That takes preparation over many passing years. This poem means to participate, is all. You can put it in your pack while adding no weight, as something you might pull out when the time is ripe. I offer it in the spirit of poetry, where words and the world meet in musicality, and as a song celebratory of walking out and walking back, with turn around time at its crux.

—*David Guterson, 2019*

OUT

1. EVERY STEP THE SAME

Here, setting out, booted, burdened,
let's suffer not to ask
about our end,
and do what we came to do:
wend.

I mean you! Before you're grass.
No sitting on it undoes fact.
Let's rise and go as trees go—
that is, with loss, and making way for light—
like trees traveling time's throw,

like stones interred,
like stars, birds, dusk, the dark,
a piped lament, a river's arc,
a hint, a dream, a moonlit ridge,
like snow or fog—let's go!

Caveat emptor—rain falls here.
We'll critique ourselves in current terms.
We'll walk beneath a shroud, a pall.
We'll lose ourselves in drapes of moss.
Contextually abroad then,

let's consume our hour's trail,
drink our fleeting compass needle,
gorge on green,
graze in streams,
make our way to that distant aerie

where the ripples in snow
say tread is query.
Such is our path,
not asked for, not left,
not traced by desire or paced by tears,

not stormed by steps or lulled by cliffs.
Leaf, mire, meal, sepal,
the breathless shadow of a casting eagle,
the bog-borne gentian incognito,
shallow lobed or deeply pleated—

this is us by sojourn kissed,
shorn of stasis, tripped.

2. THE INNER AMBLE

You say you lack the wherewithal
to slog through bends that down and up
lead nowhere except to lunch?
Doesn't that leave you stuck at the trailhead,
asking, once again, "Now what?"

Freed, then, let's clamber and climb,
regaling each other with the deep and sublime,
imagining how a plate might scour
as it grinds through time and builds up detritus,
the very slough we stride and endure,

the stuff and surface of our trod and being,
the fester of volcanoes splaying slag and waste
and leaving behind collapse in gray:
this is the color Cobain complained of
in his dour elegies and canticles.

Slot him in then between Keats and Shelley,
dead at twenty-seven, taster of ash,
Irish like Milligan and Muldoon.
Remove his name from the rolls of the gray
who suffer sciatica, crisis, corns,

the sorry blisters of overreaching,
the perpetual insistence on future brilliance,
the pain visitations and anticipations,
foremost anticipation of an end.
So up we go today,

stalwart on Little Hump,
fresh and intrepid under Mount Jupiter—
Jove, Zeus, sky king, rain lord,
conjurer of night thunder,
boundary defender—

before striking our shore between Murhut
and Cliff Creeks, dipping toes, lost to thought.

3. THE SHAMELESS THIEVES

Who can blame us? It's eight a.m.
Big Hump lies in front of us.
Saint Peters Dome waits in stately near prominence
where one might call it a redoubt or eminence.
The route up Jupiter Cliffs, it's said,

begins just left of a spring-only waterfall,
continues via chimneys and lateral ledges,
poses a crux restricted by brush,
and demands nine hours
to transcend its last difficulty.

So rare, in life, to find good beta,
route descriptions, maps of heaven,
though Trip-Report Rourke and his pard
did the west chute after fording the river
and finding flagging in the woods.

With "spicy boulder moves
but enough greenery to grovel,"
they made the summit
and repaired to a basin
where now the difficulty was patience.

"Namaste," an acolyte commented.
"Whatever your outer appearance,
I greet the soul in you."
As if those two climbers were infamously ugly.
Though it should be said there's another Saint Peters

with arresting views above Cochiti Pueblo
and a third in northwest Wisconsin.
"Did you know that?" you ask,
checking my reception here on this prominence
climbed by virtue of sundry distractions

that in truth are unsatisfactory.
In this fraught way we nurture silence,
starting with a silence never addressed
and followed by your cache of figs,
which you eat riffing on figgy pudding,

insisting I need to get with your theme,
rig my verses to swim your stream,
take a few hits at our friends the Brits
for their iffy habit of flaming it with brandy
when they might jolly well call it cake.

In short we hear voices
instead of wings
while gray jays assault your lidless fig bin,
jays on boughs set in tremulous motion
by virtue of carefully balancing bracts,

poised as they are over small, soft tips
of a downward cant or cast.
Nefarious and judicious keepers of distance,
blunt beaked, boreal, territorial, torrid,
slime mold feeders, killers, invaders,

thieves, screamers, tree-cache fillers,
they breed in winter and betray each other
with no less ruthless regard than ours,
and yet we applaud them as they limit our estrangement
or for regaling us with beggary and pomp.

Away temporarily from our many useful gadgets,
we turn to jays for a modicum of merriment,
sugarcoating these cutthroat survivors
with another brand or form of loss:
all those lone friendless moments in the woods

redeemed by the silence of gray jays.
"Wing on!" you say, churlish as ever,
guarding your figs from clever forays,
arguing "limited availability"
and adding to it "commodious taste—

Turkish figs, organic and nutritious,
derived from a Smyrna cultivar."

4. WILD RHODODENDRONS

Are you mad at me for this?
We'll sit at removes, then, turned toward no sun,
silent together, talking about ourselves—
whether we ought to look at each other,
whether an amble or a slap is called for,

whether a cease-fire respite is warranted,
whether our downhill run should be fretful.
With these and like-minded importunings
we could gather ourselves
for a tour of rhododendrons,

which today, as always, present leggy fretwork
as if with no event or muster,
as if to say they can speak for themselves
without any need for threat or bluster,
always delicate in their charms.

They're come as you are,
comme ci, comme ça,
here and not here, drapery, walls,
often little more than hillside scraggle
or weak-burned, clear-cut, poor, bedraggled,

or lofting trailside froth.
This, our state flower,
lacks density and power,
takes too willingly to its minimal consequence,
makes no bargains with reputation,

doesn't pretend to live up to promise,
and endures raw scorn for its willingness
to disappoint without going out on a limb.
Eaten by beavers, it flowers in clusters,
plundered by marauders, it fails to thrive.

Kudos to our heath, in short,
not for its fortnight's pinkish munificence
but for its far more general recalcitrance
and incidence. This is a thing you like about us,
how we so often get it all wrong—

Rhododendron macrophyllum, after all,
for a bush of long greens and no thorns.

5. THE WEIGHT OF WINDFALL

Spare me, I reply, from niggling correctness,
and get on with our inimitable, indifferent switchbacks
reminding us of fresh limitations.
With bushwhacking, sidestepping,
flanking and chiding.

With each fresh step
in the scheme of our wending.
Fallén trees in whimsical geometries
will lend to our woods
their comic trajectories with humor

more epic than the brisk fits of squirrels,
who are, by comparison, vaudevillians.
One must admire their instant reversals,
disingenuous flimflamming starts,
and most marvelous of all how some seem to fly

at four o'clock in the morning.
These autumn midden builders, truffle nibblers,
and trail greeters punchily arrest
our forward progress with their brief but demanding
performances on logs

or by scrabbling and spiraling over bark.
Star turns in bit parts, you breezily assess,
while making a pitch for windfall en masse
as superior to my scampering farce.
We must weigh, then, the weight of things together,

and whether words are equal to our task,
and whether to loll in heaps by the river
finishing the rich, dense figs from Smyrna,
cloying as they are in my estimation,
dessert figs someone fobbed off on you

at Christmas, a pass-along pack, regifted.
This is other people, you say,
then rail against all the liars in your life,
those who disappointed you once
versus those who disappointed you twice:

the frank, snide, sour pretenders
with whom you'd never take a hike.

6. FINER ENDS

We're silenced by that at Five Mile Camp,
astride our winter river with our feet up on rocks,
seething as always with thoughts and opinions,
waving at our world a categorical wand
or succumbing to torpor or fueled by reverie

or thinking, again, about the glory of lunch:
do you suppose we should trot out our sandwiches now
as a means to make better sense of it all,
and in the spirit of an expected anticlimax?
The way ahead doesn't speak for itself—

firs, cedars, lichens, boulders,
each totemic element of our scene
foreseen, forsworn, yet here again.
This is our waking and walking impression,
our native, tired, green formulation—

the names of things as if to say,
there's more to a name than a name.
That's why I ask, in a devil's club bog,
for silence to speak with far less gravity
and for the names of things

to take emptiness as their form,
though if the apogee poets are poets of silence,
how—a technicality—would we know it?
According to Trappists, sign language is golden,
unlike their chaliced, holy ale;

by labor of hands do they get us in our cups;
strong for the monk, weak for the nun,
this for their blood, this for their brothers,
this for pilgrims, this for export.
Such silence accords with our natural ends

and is falsely discerned in the nought between thoughts
as we cross a runnel on slipshod cobbles,
decidedly unacrimonious for once
and taking the long view and the short route.
Our cumulative effort is neurotically efficient;

we're driven by desire to pare down exhaustion,
to join shortest lines with minimal swivel,
to shoot the middle in the manner of Italians
driving fast cars through hills.
That's the logic of tedious travel.

One must shorten each bend by direction.
Following curves twines counter to our ends.
Taught by that stingy teacher, fatigue,
we learn to find ourselves perpetually abroad
in that dark wood where the wavering way costs.

We walk, by hours, with discernment born of rigor,
although I should add that today's middle path
calls for middling extremities of force.
Our discipline hones soft, our line is least resistant.
There's nothing to be gained, legs tensed, on a tightwire.

And we ought to expect this truth of existence:
that slides, heaved roots, fallen trees, and cutbanks
inevitably interpose and have a voice.
Are you with me?
Because this many miles into our trip

we take shifts as laggards or bounding ahead,
leapfrogging one another at rest,
forwarding our theories of forward motion
by enacting displays of phony vigor
addressed to the flagger with ragged breath.

Such petty forays inform much of living.
They weigh us down with their inward drivel
and hammer home our piggish souls.
In sum, on we go, always shy of hope,
perpetually stopping short of deferring,

under a pressure and pall of our making,
eating ourselves, by anxiety, into thinness
and never drinking from the font of self-forgiveness.
Crimped by tight laces, we ache and rail,
bloodless, enervated, we plod through our paces;

our stride is wrong no matter its length,
our gait, short or long, is another walker's gait,
our rhythm is lost altogether.
Strange to ourselves, we're hampered
and hindered, and worse, we're largely willful

to contend where we ought to breathe
such forest air as induces finer ends.

7. MY OWN INCESSANT VOICE-OVER

Perforce does sweat in a cold wood breed.
At odds, divided, we part with our shadows.
They travel in congress, lose voice and regress,
intimate nothing, offer no language,
descend into depths without fair warning

or hover over the crests of hills
on the far side of troubling chasms.
Here each river runs to itself
with a certain concentricity of whirl,
as if a propulsive throb of the earth

in clockwise wheeling turns was imparted.
A quake can move our world off its axis—
a paroxysm clenching with measurable wobble—
and change our grid by cataclysmic inches;
over time, then, truth is forked over

the way a slow gardener forks dirt.
Even the poles must flip at intervals
we refuse to defer to or even consider;
even the Needles and Sawtooth Ridge
are other than serrated peaks.

And if they're just upthrusts
from the Lower Tertiary
in a territory of weak metamorphosis,
then why, friend, are we bitter today
with familiar, silent dissension and disquiet,

as if to say time is endless?
Why do I hear, in the mean mind's ear,
"Don't ask me again to identify that plant
as elderberry or not?"
My desire insists on desiring to desire

and will not stop to embrace your awe
of dirt on snow or wind-torn needles.
I prefer my thought solo on tracks and branches.
I want private witness while wracking this forest
of assorted and relentless present desiderata.

I'll take this world today without your monologue
and am perfectly capable of blanching its features
with my own incessant voice-over.
Or of missing it.
But for now, in a slant of sun, sharing almonds,

we loll like lovers.
This is the time to revisit our trip description.
Neither of us mentions current elevation.
Moods and caprice hold sway in this bend
where soon you snore beneath your hat brim,

leaving me to swallow my loneliness.
Here all my silent interstices come together
as noisy fabric lifted into madness
by a shaker flexing the corners of thought
in erratic but well-timed whips.

But as they say, "we are here
as on a darkling plain,"
where suffering's volitional but not pain.
Is that the best we can do today,
in our tired practice of pith and verities?

Are homilies dead? Is everyone wrong,
not least of all you, partly because you're long
in the tooth and lacking a ready answer?
Maybe you and I had better keep walking
with your shaky knees and my vinegar.

With our copious planning and ample gear,
our rain pants and water filters.

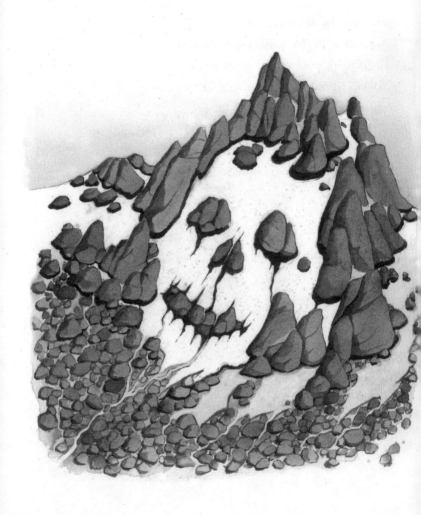

8. OLD SNOW

Old snow today is akin to a tray
that carries evidence of winter.
Ravaged, stained, dimpled, traipsed,
it shrinks in shade as if to say
it isn't done with living.

It hasn't had enough of being.
It regrets spring's defeat,
clings but shrinks, rejects acceptance.
There's nothing to be gained
via early acquiescence, no good or grace

in melting. Old snow's opposed to everything
and never hails a brighter future.
Instead its dents and cavities darken.
Morose in March but gone by April,
it's replaced by goat shit, veronica, and lichen.

In other words, these last dregs are inching back
and dragging it out before going.
Steeping the last of their tea out of habit
even when spring has gone rabid.
Indeed, snow's pernicious

to the wrong sort of witness
and may be so much locked-up water
finding its way toward freedom.
Disparate dreams of melting, then,
but still we must take our words

where we find them.
The world must be framed and furnished,
after all, with its fading snow
either failing or redeemed
by virtue of restless interpretation.

We give it a verse lest we abrogate,
but meantime we have to watch it go
while offering opinions
or conjuring conceits
or listening to our thoughts rephrase themselves.

And who's in charge of these sundry misconceptions?
What other option do we have in talking
unless we learn, like poets of silence,
not to sing of this world again?
I'll hold my tongue, then, for half a line,

so old snow can slip in sideways
unadorned and unaddressed.

9. A RESPITE BEYOND THE CURVE

And this is river travel, with the present always arriving
and leaving laden with rabid commentary.
With errant proclivities, with hues and perplexities.
But I made no promises at our trailhead, yes?
Never said we'd halt under cliffs

or at a likely spot to change our socks.
I made no prologue and mentioned no crag,
no lakelet charmed showed on my map,
I aimed at nothing, not even a bivouac,
which you would criticize as is your wont,

poised at sign-in with your walking stick
honed to a crevice-catching point,
testing it for rebound while I'm bent and lacing up,
there before I'm there with your gloves
and greased anorak, immune to censure

and packing moleskin, enough for a platoon,
and iodine tablets that turn water acrid,
and your blackened flint and steel in a ditty bag.
In short I detest your constant assessment
and deplore your "suggestions" about changing

the kit I carry, my tackle and trim,
the cut and cross of my straps and buckles.
I won't engage in debate again
on the latter-day, flexing, sternum-strap feature
versus the tried-and-true, storied tumpline.

It doesn't matter if you're ahead or behind,
I won't give you this this once or concede
that, together, we're going somewhere or not.
Mute wrath's our field today
while we quarter under mountains darker

than your emptiness and more obscure.
The vault of air and textured space
is cold if we compare
and scalds us empty under naked stars,
but here we wear the shroud of self

and, battered bare, crouch together
under flimsy shelter, fellows well met
with tea and pilot bread, quips
and a German camp stove. Your presence says—
I take this back—the old charade's expired.

For the nonce, in jest, all dead, all rot,
as you have gone from walking tall
to wavering and bent. I see you there,
an old stone savage armed with old-school English
and leaning on your stick the way Brits do

for advantage or effect, dependent, now,
on tonsorial skills and vim,
dependent on the salt still in your gait
but reduced, redacted, defenestrated,
and daunted by reports from doctors

on the state of your pulse:
to you, all of this I remove
while we steep damp tea in our haven.
And since the ground's damp too, we'll take our repast
on plastic bags in yore dismissed as unpoetic.

Their many shimmering folds
are needle furrowed, et cetera.
Their rippling din in wind, et cetera.
Our kettle's keening boil, et cetera.
This malady of words extends,

theoretically, to all, ad nauseam.
I come round again to asking questions.
Which for you is humbug, furbelow, and fiddle-faddle,
bunk best left to the end-game knackerman,
mental effluvium that doesn't bear a flummox,

red herrings executing a seizure on our hummock.
The question for you is the weight of our hardtack
and your memory however gratuitous of Sailor Boy,
otherwise known in your idiom as dog biscuit.
Let's not fret as we argue about this,

here in our lair with oolong and text,
drying musty socks draped on sticks.
Which way is it then?
Consider a bird bone with its struts
before you answer.

Or a goldthread's sepals
or the wing beats of mosquitoes.
The way things are is a good place to start,
though certain smart people will tell you not.
At any rate, the upshot is, our fate as travelers

is to up the ante
and take the step undermined by scree,
the slope in extremis, the icy dart,
and execrable exposure to exposure.
That's less compelling than pilot bread, you counter,

with its complement of flaccid, dubious calories,
good for nothing but a dunk by a fool
taking heart from dust at trailside.
It's just you and me in our wallow of moss,
though accompanied by weariness

such that we two salts
don't give a damn about the meaning of it all.
What matters is a trailside balm
and the recognition of equality in acts—
for example, that refuge in Sailor Boy biscuits

is an equal metaphysic to doing dishes.
Fortunately or not, then, our teapot cleans
with a swirl, dries with a whip.
Our hardtack endures, your analgesic kicks in.
One of those moments far too brisk

for which we'll pay in listlessness later.
But still I shoulder my pack with a flip,
a skyward rotation and self-conscious shift,
rich with such dangerous self-regard
as governs the temper of our aging.

Seventy's the new twenty in advertisement,
with amenities, upgrades, and a cozening silver burnish,
though neither of us has a watch today,
believing, as we do, that it's fair to read the sun
even in the dark of these woods. Is that wisdom

and if not, will we know it when we feel it?
The appropriate conundrum—our human punishment—
is that trapped in our parts
we can't see us how they see us.
Our wisdom could be doddering cant

or the good-money-after-bad mad rant
of the permanently committed.

10. WOODLAND TRAIL-TROLL
BERSERKER DEVIL-BEAR

We move ahead and in a swale are hailed
by a pilgrim waltzing east who claims a dozen caches
and a secret knowledge of distant passes—
a broad and bearded bloke bedecked
in what looks to be a hair shirt or a burlap tunic,

a jug swung from hemp twine at his hip,
his load like a hunchback,
his tongue swollen dark—strangler of words—
his jib jittery, his slouch hat jarred,
his mood blue, his girth and gout

both outsized and amenable
to a younger man's mythic treatment.
He proffers irreverent bons mots on "poontang,"
warns us not to laugh at facts,
asks for scag, but jokingly,

combs his greasy, protean locks
and declares he's Scottish and a Pict.
What have we read of late that's great? he japes,
then lets blow with a goodly gob of snot
aimed in a blast past your head.

"Field guides," you supply. "Treatises on wings.
A socialist exegesis on screech owl pellets.
Annals of daylight. Water testimonials.
A history of pikas. Annotated pollen."
"Puh!" he retorts, in spittle and mirth.

"Snoggerdog and balderdash!
Rot, trash, tripe, twaddle!
Turgid fustian and bombastriousness!
Pompous, puffed-up trailside trifles!"
Our eastbound Robert Bly–brand brute

insists your list's a fencer's feint
fobbed off on him
from insecurities of intellect and reading.
He won't let you hedge with minor humor;
he's stern in asserting your sulking irony

results from not growing up.
Who is this bedeviled, phlegm-inflected geezer?
How long are we to stand with heavy packs
while he rolls out one-upmanship
and mishmash?

By what possessed is this crank's spirit?
Odiferous with duff and decomposition,
hmmphing, weathered, sparged, catarrhed,
he leaches, thaws, tills, consolidates, plows,
cleaves, dissolves, groans, breathes in grist

and breathes out loam,
regales the toothsome cauliflower mushroom,
the admirable bolete, and the violet cortinarius,
unbidden sings his fungal prescriptions
with manifold exhortations and bewares—

"No beetle boreholes, stand-up pores"—
probes for us a fulsome shelf fungus
redolent when cooked of *stringozzi al limone*,
and produces from his pocket
a warted giant puffball

the size of an English Premier League football
·but in the style of a French illusionist.
"*Calbovista subsculpta*," you say,
nose deep in your dear guide to fungi,
"the somewhat sculptured bald foxfart."

Our woodland trail-troll berserker devil-bear—
our cyclops green man *Waldgeist* satyr—
our howling Iron John *kodama* yeti—
our Rooster Cogburn windigo warrior—
is a hulking undaunted golem familiar

and a screaming Jungian animus figure
with no time for infantile snickering at flatulence
and no time for subtler-than-thou
shenanigans of the sort you're wont to employ.
All of this we can't leave behind

when at last our mutual farewells are delivered,
as certain lowbrow horror sequels year after year persevere.
And while our fern-crowned forest paterfamilias
pounds his cantankerous way toward the river
you give him a long mock-trembling finger

with your signature antic, ersatz assurance
before acknowledging, yes, you're scared.

11. DO BATS EXIST?

Give us our walk, then, in the hour before twilight.
Show us the way though witching's nigh.
Grant us the courage to thwart dour spirits.
Explain the libido of low serotonin.
Ask your Valkyries to dole out instead

the humblest ration of Christ's daily bread.
Better yet, with light leaving living,
help us to stumble on a rationale for walking,
guide us swiftly to God's cocktail hour.
Plead with Him our case for dry kindling

and deliver us from nada, please, with a little cup
from your wondrous and excellent deus ex machina
espresso machine.
This, those, and like supplications
inform our late-day slog and march

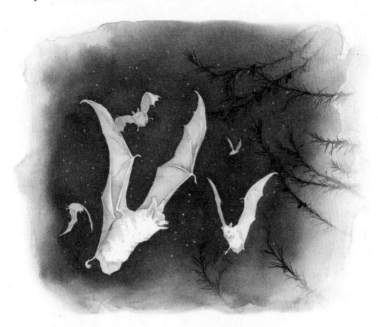

toward where precisely for a camp in the forest?
And none of your Old Paar pickiness, please,
none of your dotage or codgerly pondering
of every flat's drainage in this late gloaming.
Your gravelly meander's counter to sopor,

your dithering's adverse to our nocturnal succor.
To wit, let's run up a stay against wee hours
free of your muddle and sluggishness.
Let's say to life in darkness, *bueno*,
we'll make it safely to the bight-bay of morning.

Hold your sidling sighing, then,
and point out a place I can gamely go at it
while you mourn the *di*verse ills of choice
in that wattled neck of your internal forest.
Fie and a literary pox on you, goat beard!

I'm putting up our tent as shepherds do
in the austere Absaroka Range lees—
that is, with crossing sticks outstretched
on a relatively level plane.
I'm busy boiling our grub on a flame,

even as you loiter over annotated poetry
and precious nature guide errata.
"The bat," you say, "is felt, not seen,
inferred from hints overhead, soft flits,
from rustling spirals that might be else,

from downdrafts, flutters, surges, quivers,
agitations, sudden shivers,
intimated by nighttime shudders,
a billowing surmise in deeper darkness,
a bare suggestion never lit,

a guess on wings, a wavering waft,
a punctuated roiling somewhere aloft,
a switching shadow in a canopy's matrix,
a ripple, plummet, streak, disappearance,
here but not here, gone by definition.

The bat," you add, "is mostly projection,
although you will find them feet up in caves,
corporeal as us, asleep, just hanging,
or see them in moonlight, punctuating air,
inverse fireflies, dark ink quicksilver.

The hoary bat 'appears' at vesper
with a warm-up prayer for sluggish mosquitoes
or—if a broad-footed Yuma myotis—
works slow water after dark invocations.
One must imagine them in their hours of torpor

meditating upside down on life
while shunning this strange, lit world."

12. WHO GOES THERE?

We're in our home where we've made it;
we've carried and outlaid it.
We're hearth and sofa, tea and wafers,
but also miners of multifarious voices
that incense and dwell in we two campers

pregnant with Jack Daniel's and cannabis.
Or so you claim as you fete your chef
with narrative blather and endlessness.
And as layabouts now, fire-provoked,
we report to each other certain ghosts

of warriors advancing by screams
in our dread-drenched forest.
These visitations and deep night panics
signify how firmly the undead live
as shifting quibbles between marred shadows,

as entreaties and unexplained whims.
Up they come, painted in blood,
as clamor unstemmed by the Mouth of Hell,
as chiller tales devised by spliffs,
as midnight's rush toward insanity.

The dark side, they say, is limbic in its axis
and has no need for theory or praxis,
taking what it needs from the prefrontal cortex
where schizophrenia lashes out.
Who is that out there in the dead-of-night stream?

What comes walking, if haltingly—
who goes there?
What is that knell so poly-discordant?
Who makes music in the death of our slumber?
What is that barbarous, darker chorus

playing always farther out in the forest?
Tonight we must be blinded by embers
and open to ravage and attack by dirge;
tonight you'll have your charnel-ground tremors
and I my goring, ghastly dream:

the surreal tale of the hiker impaled
by a no-bullshit billy on a windy ridge,
the starved cougar's assaulting incisors,
the bear, the wolf, the Trailside Slayer,
the desultory hiker met on a bridge.

We'll scare ourselves with voices from our river
and with the music of our sunless sphere.
We'll be travelers sequestered,
poised at each chamber,
scribing with cursive speed our dreams

before they're lost in the mirror.
And from the north, tonight, falls Demon Creek,
gathered together from unnamed tarns
unseen on an unnamed ridge.
In fingers all our forces come together

and run downhill toward larger rivers
that disembowel darker canyons. We'll go there
together. Furtively we'll peruse those burial grounds
where butterflied limbs are left for buzzards,
flayed with an attentive interest in economy

by those who've vanquished, like coroners,
what's morbid. Someone has to do it, after all.
We'll go in that or some other fashion
while the forensic pathologist eats lunch
with his feet up, matter-of-fact as Hamlet's gravedigger.

"Whose grave's this, sirrah?" "Mine, sir."
Just think of the steadily drumming obits
we've duly hmmed and daily gawped at—
the violin virtuoso haunted by addiction,
the gifted preacher who spoke for tolerance,

the courtly dean of Washington's press corps,
the famous foodie, Audrey Hepburn.
At best we're briefly deepened or offended,
at worst and probably more frequently distracted.
We haven't yet finished the crossword puzzle

or determined to act on the odds at the Preakness.
We haven't read our maps beneath headlamps.
We haven't knelt by our river with dishes
and heard between rocks the Reaper's edge lifted.
Always our jig is up somewhere hence;

now's too early in perpetuity.
Who doesn't plan on plodding tomorrow
or step around shit on the way to the gallows
with a view toward saving even mediocre shoes
on loan from his executioner?

God's groaning pews are full of disbelievers
while the woods at night stage Beelzebub
in splendor, Moloch, Belial, Dagon, Osiris,
and *The Texas Chainsaw Massacre*.
At least we're here with torches and sugar,

charades, barbs, quips, Twenty Questions,
scintillating fauna descriptions, divertimento
and scabrous badinage, purple memories,
plaintive screeds, lists of best bad songs
from the seventies,

memories of meaningful moments from analysis,
rationales for not ending it all,
and your nasal celebration of Hank Williams Sr.
delivered into the abyss.
Thus we trend toward that *petite mort*, slumber,

in our tent world teeming with night insurrections.
Which bardo will we cross this eve?
Which apparition will possess our attention?
The host of players you've tamped in low places
will have its day as dark descends.

DON'T LOOK BACK say the signs in this forest,
so go ahead and tease out bread,
each wad's cause and effect.
And one last tip:
carve your signifying blaze into trunks

as, when your dream's forgot,
such markers stand as telling first impressions.
They're code for all your lode in strata.
But now my toll has rung for two a.m.
and in waking sleep I've gradually found

no beginning, no middle,
no end.

BACK

1. TURN AROUND TIME

Hey!
Get your boots laced up again,
dispense, dispense, dispense!
Finish your toilet, bury that bolus—
embrace, embrace, embrace!

The world's flaming and shaking today,
counter, original, spare, strange,
even if we've changed.
Suck down your tea, then,
tuck in your gruel, you and I must move.

Our tent's struck, our line's undone,
we've heard enough from you.
There's even sun, or some, for once,
though overnight, I give it, true,
your nature guide got chewed.

Look already, up from text,
scrutinize our sky with zest:
move, move, move!
Our peregrination stakes an obvious claim
to reverence—rapt—and attention!

Though it ought to be added
that our northern coordinates
have been under water
through multiple eras
the length, more or less, of one stanza.

In other words, we have to start home,
though it's not the end of the hike for us,
finito, taps, or kaddish.
There's wood rush and pinedrops,
we'll make something of them;

we'll tarry, unhurried, I promise.
We'll maintain a quieter, afternoon joy,
at worst—just a little—feel mired.
Because of late I've heard your knelling note,
your susurrus, your crackling pyre.

You look at me as if to say
you're terminally, infirmly tired,
a slipping treadmiller,
an expirer in rictus.
So wake and walk, dear confidante,

let's sign off, make trail. Watch deer strip lichen
and nibble nubs, towhead baby, old-man's beard;
such fodder speaks the world to me,
but about that I'm wary of feeling pleased,
and just as surely greet my destroying angel

whether in partial or universal veil,
whether sunlit or delicate in leaf meal.
You say you wouldn't nibble a hooded false morel?
Would never ruffle a common deer truffle?
Delete all recipes for toothed jelly fungus?

Have no truck with the short-stemmed russula?
Okay. Your lover's quarrel with the world
remains a quarrel, then.
We won't search for them in understory.
We'll follow, instead, your safer tributary

until it leads to negation in a final river.
To where our ever closer look yields mortal jitters.
So excuse me amid my fried chicken mushrooms
and for staining myself with bleeding mycena,
for gray pig's ears on a shelf in winter,

for every impostor lying amid buttons,
for black trumpet mushrooms
with ambiguous funnels,
and for the free-gilled jack-o'-lantern
you ate for dinner.

Let's walk instead strained convexities
between hogbacks
laid down by winter melt and drainage,
let's leave behind all fungal fear
and make, instead, slick cobble crossings.

And I can't remember these switchbacks either,
because going up and coming down—
neither is familiar.
Such tight reversals deride and remind us:
we don't belong in this or other weather.

Cliff face cuts occasion toe bang,
by dint of roots and rocks we fade.
Down we go toward home together,
splayed and voicing ligamentous complaints
as if they weren't just something we make,

suffering on top of pain.
Our slant's precipitous—an unfair gradient—
our drop's a drag if we don't sing,
and louder sing for tatters in our dress,
but meanwhile, I guess, I have to ache,

because this zigzaggery's
got doglegs and hairpins
enough to make me ask what's in a name
over many long miles of miner's plod
with a mule, a bottle,

and a need for entertainment,
a need, in short, to amuse by designation.

2. A TRAIL LIKE THIS

As such we climb the Devils Staircase,
try Ex-Spire, mount the Incisor,
ponder the Sundial and Infinity Tower,
the Bandersnatch, Cats Ears,
Horses Mouth, Noodle Needle,

Hermes, Bears Breast, Rottenrockel Spitz,
Fag Crag, the Royal Shaft.
Oh spirited, old-school, golden band of brothers,
give us more novel tags in knickers,
be merry and devil-may-care on slopes,

cut rakishly in robust woolen robe,
perform the circumstances' proper glissade,
and lean on that long-handled ice ax of yours
while godlike you brand your ascents.
This is the old Euro-purist's way.

A claim's made without a miner's lament.
But as for us, our interest is no longer in distinction.
We've been tenderized by time, our copper's annealed,
our leather's cauterized, our wounds slowly heal
if at all they heal—I for one am scarred, gnarled,

blanched, blotched, can't be put right with a rag
and a polish, won't take a comeback refurbish.
Yet I'm willing to dog it with my inside foot planted
and a will not to cut or refute the schemata.
In me a certain late torque prevails

that, when I lock it down,
the rust breaks a little and moves ahead
the eroded threads for a day or two,
for which I'll pay. Me?
I'm free-floating cartilage waiting for gout

but meanwhile at rest between root forks.
I'm switchback addlepated, by turns overheated,
dizzied by indecisive circuits.
Undulations have thrown me for a loop,
alternations dash my compass.

There's no end to my ambivalence or tacks,
and I feel soon enough, on a trail like this,
the something always fundamentally amiss,
the imbalance inherent in the inner ear's labyrinth,
the *mal de débarquement* that's apparently our lot

even minus the sea and a ship.
Haven't you, too, had enough of bends?
Didn't you hope for a little less flexion
and a little less constant change of direction,
fewer corners, pivots, hooks,

a cognizable trend, no pirouettes,
a God who doesn't always suggest
that turnabout's fair play, you should accept?
Such shifting wend could well play out
to an end if we defer and let it.

We could navigate between negation and grace
and then find out we were wrong or right;
we could oscillate like light waves or insulin,
like Foucault's pendulum.
So I ask for a break and take it—a respite.

Here I'll attend to my dampening chagrin.
I'll sprawl and wince.
Here my urge to stop must win.
So open your book and look at it instead,
I'll leave you with your dogwood minutiae,

your Tweedy's lewisia, your miner's lettuce,
while I treat my assorted infirmities and diseases,
my maladies and my banes.
I'm fatally unsound,
let that ring through our forest,

let that join the ever-massing chorus
of humanity's long complaint.
An elegy for me, please,
within the larger lament—
is that too much to ask, and you say, "Yes."

Well, the peach you dared to eat
has gone the way of rockabilly pompadours
and you and I, we're lame.
I've got an ankle like my uncle's,
I sag, I'm ashamed, but anyway let's press ahead

before the Footman changes his mind or snickers.
We're drawn back from whence
we were once expectorated
into the mouth of our dreams with missteps,
bowing to our trail's involutions,

treading but braced by walking poets
opening our way.

3. A NARROW ROAD TO THE INTERIOR

They say the key to walking well is joy,
not pain relief, but who are they?
Since joy could rout us from the trail later
and a switchback implies a return.
A cautionary shrink might say much production

leads surely to dearth, and therefore, pilgrim,
walk undeterred, keep to the middle way.
We'll go that way among diverse "walks"—
this way, tall, on, away, on by, on the wild side,
on sunshine, the line, with me, the dog, on water,

like a man, in Memphis, it off, on the moon—
we'll walk it as they walk the PCT,
in highly recommended shoes.
But as for you, you've put bad money
on a nonexistent filly, need something newer,

lack endurance for a downturn.
Your load's cinched but insecure,
unbalanced for traverse, lopsided, top-heavy.
"Now what?" is your mantra;
you don't believe in progress.

Where's the end, then?
Are we to walk from here to there
and back again for no good reason?
I gave your guidebook to a callow traveler,
a lad I met on a path to a promontory,

but he never sent it back
despite demanding my return address.
I'm a disappointment to you;
I cross a basin in silence when an ice field's imminent.
I linger in cirques, keep an eye out for snags,

if bear grass is elk-cropped I speak to that.
If blazes mark our path I protest, rebut:
"Prior travelers are prone to forays,
which is why they flag or chip their errors.
Life's full of great mistakes.

Way leads on to way. Turning back's a terror.
The lost are mostly loath to climb
and prone to go on giving elevation
until, too late, they're in an unknown drainage."
Such while we guess and stumble

on the traipse between one meadow and the next,
or stop to genuflect in a nave of moss
or in a slough of sloughs, in side channels, in backwaters.
There's no river here except the mind of river,
where as usual we bushwhack ahead while harmless;

that's one way.
You hold the whiplike branch until I'm through,
refrain from lash, and leave the rest—so what's our rule?
Job suggested, "Ask the beasts,"
but then there's Dōgen: "He who doubts that mountains

walk does not yet understand his own walking."
I propose, therefore, a narrow road to the interior,
where there are cliffs to pass before our hearts
are laid asunder or unravel. "In summer mountains
bow to holy high-water clogs, bless this long journey,"

wrote Bashō. And who are we to disagree
with his asymmetries? The how-to books are shipped
to younger people whose discretionary cash remains
at issue. They make a bargain with the future,
put it off until tomorrow, whereas our boots are treated

in advance of conditions and with a view toward mud
and purgatory. Like me you're looking forward to dinner.
Big thoughts haunt you with too much persistence.
Our woods now feel like someone else's.
We came to the river and, dejected, looked in,

but late glacial till turned the current to a surface,
a scrim that's a bath for our debris and not a mirror,
a gush amniotic and—ask Narcissus—useless.
Too late to take a baptism, don't you think?
Because such a going-under's

estranged from our condition.
You and I must find a bridge or boat,
either one's all right with me, I come and go,
then change my mind; just keeping options open,
the Way of Vacillation.

I'm walking both ways, I'm on my feet
decrying ambiguity for its own sake,
then hailing it, then calling it cheating—
but that's just me.
There's nothing safe to say while walking,

nothing we won't take back one day.
The trail without naysayers is found far between,
the route around, or through, is blocked by trees.
On our trail, what's inevitable?
There's coming and going,

breathing and danger,
waste, hunger, worry, leaving.
There's feeling unloved by definition
through all manner of encounter,
bypass, and deference.

There's moving aside, down, up, maybe, or not,
as gestures of aggression—
even we can't say for certain.
There's condemning and expecting condemnation.
But as for you, beauty's opportunity for pain

and prompts such censure aimed at age
as subverts our trip—if for a second.

4 . THE GOATHERD

"Let's go," you urge, "as goatherds go,
since herders go where goats go
and nowhere else especially.
Might we be followers?
Might we vivify a lack of sole direction?

I'm fine with B to A undesignated
and would pipe midday at the shrine to Pan,
doze guiltlessly, my point to have no plan
and let goats dictate."
To which the goatherd answers:

"I see that and this trail of telling turds
joining other turds across these mountains,
and trails joining trails toward the lowest passes,
south slopes offering richer grass where rocks
abut to shelter us from wind and rain.

I'll tuck in there for an hour or more
as is my duty in the course of herding,
which you can take or leave—
anyway, I'll sleep, leaving you those things
of which you speak with great intensity,

but let me point out, too, for your sake,
the location of a spring whose waters prove.
I'll rest and dream of leonine tarts,
drink, sup, take my ease,
there's bound of course to be one or two

get taken down by ky-yoats, so be it,
what am I to do, stay tuned all day?
The wily must eat, that's well-known,
and told in all the bestiary tales.
Which include my lewdness soon,

my lonely animalia, and, with years, a chin wisp
and a tail, until this innocent's pastoral is
a flowing font for broad disgust.
I'll go goatish on you indubitably; I'll have my rut.
Today's delight in whistle and wending

is, tomorrow, my horn, emptied.
I know what you don't—
nothing, exactly.
In other words, don't look to me for advice
on lore. Lost, lost, lost!"

Thus this goat-boy, whose way is just to be—
to put it that way's your admiring inclination,
but each day's wind and vista,
dog and staff, *maa*, bleat, kid giving fits,
billy banter, nanny chatter—

enough to make me a stockbroker
instead on the 6:10 in from Hampstead
that, reaching Charing Cross,
lets no goats on board
or shitting past the turnstiles.

So please. Let's walk today as if we mean it
and leave behind your armchair dream of goatherd peace.

5. MADONNA OF THE BOGACHIEL

Your idyll's wishful thinking
and your meadow nymphs and mountain naiads
drive you down a trail quick.
You're just a lusty satyr drained, no wick,
a rogue whose curd's up,

spent by time's dint,
a wether, a ball-less bucca.
Just don't go feral on me, please,
I'd like to be home by eight
with a glass of tea beside me,

watching TV, the Nature Channel, preferably,
which according to you should feature,
each night, a walk on the wild side:
the mating-season secrets of keen mountain goats,
he and she, mounting and mounted:

do you have a different subject, please?
Or will you still pursue your claim that mounting
surmounts all from death to picket fences?
If so, I'll stuff my ears again while we're in tandem.
I'll press ahead while at my back you flog your thesis.

If I'm not buggered by your walking stick
I'll fit my mind to something else
as you persist in this, your font of meaning.
Okay, fine, mountain lions do it six hundred times
in forty hours, then split,

whereas spinner dolphins wile away their days
in pod-wide orgies, diddling and kissing,
deploying fin and flipper.
What was that? I missed it.
All business, which is not to say

you're not an interesting informant
on the ways of things in nature,
the joining strategies of hoof and claw—
to you, that's poetry, and so I guess it has to be
for me as well, since who can separate?

Go ahead, then, with your train of coupling couplets,
I'll convert them to my ends,
divertissement, no impediment,
I'll keep the track beneath my boots and pen
as I am on a roll today while you're salacious.

Giddy with word flower,
you invoke the muse of male bards:
you call Astarte, you hear her summons
to the pool above the white-water run-out of no return,
a ragged drift that has to end

where logs will drag you down
and rip your muscle walls apart
in preparation for an entrail reading.
Even as you call her name
our way is disappearing.

You say you've seen the smile
on the face of the Madonna.
She was dwelling on the Bogachiel
with a damp book and a hammock,
collecting drinking water from her tarp

and chewing licorice.
This, she said, was how to wait out rain
without discomfort, but what you wanted
was the secret of her immaculate confection.
"What can I get?" was your sole question.

Just ask the solo muse of River Bogachiel,
thirty miles up in winter, net suspended,
speaking tersely, unavailable
except as a projection—
is that a woman you would manage?

Observation is its own agenda, friend.
These woods, frankly, are full of Eves
and witches running through your filter.
Not a moment passes without their crowning stature.
That's the cast of things for you on this primeval circuit.

But I watch your back and you watch mine,
grades and contours coming at us one by one
in plodding process, and meanwhile all these thirsts
of your devising not to mention otherwise,
like a root or rock that means to catch us unaware

and end it all when we were focused
on a pack adjustment.

6. LARKIN'S LAMENT

I suppose that's why some walkers have a footwear fetish.
The provenance of last on which their boots are built,
their heel counters keeping off the grandest *mal* of all
and, in case of injury, the finer seaming points
of basket-weave ankle-taping therapy.

Again I ask, who wants to walk the final few
with a gimp in this,
the age of selective serotonin reuptake inhibitors?
Flood your brain in gold stars instead,
from a loving teacher.

Learn the Low-Dye wrap for heel spurs,
the anchor strap and twist for turf toe chronic,
and closely monitor your callus accretion:
you never know when, instead of something else
you believed in or anticipated,

it's mere dead skin that's fatal.
Are you lulled a bit by this our question?
If so, that's commensurate with our condition,
with waking up each day aghast at more perdition.
I know a man who plans each hike

before the last one's through,
never takes a trip past which a question slips
if he can stop it; he's eighty-two.
Does that negate our walking issues?
I'd like to know because I'm losing my resolve

and feel a blister coming on,
there's a dampness at my back
that's soaking through. I've lost my clip,
I think, in nascent shin splints,
and can't see how to limp in character this afternoon.

It doesn't help, this nattering you're up to,
asking me to stay the course at your disposal,
demonstrating once again your mountaineering rest step
and urging syncopation on our gait.
Are we, in fact, going one direction, you and I,

with a united predilection?
Maintaining access to a shrinking pool
of favorable experiences—
should I want that, like you?
You keep on doing what the English do—

crossing turnstiles, closing gates,
map against your chest in rainproof case,
an hour after dusk five courses at an inn
and later, port, wafers, and a blaze.
What's more, your walking stick's a godlike rod

to which there's no refute.
You: "Henry David's said it all on walking."
Hail, fellow, well met, in transcendental innocence,
but let's not forget that Woolf joined the Ouse
after, "What greater delight and wonder

can there be than to leave the straight lines
of personality and deviate into those footpaths
that lead beneath brambles and thick tree trunks
into the heart of the forest where live those wild beasts,
our fellow men?" Indeed we fear Virginia,

you and me. We have a lovely view of trees,
take repast in a glade—tinned anchovies and cheese—
drink gladly from streams, enjoy both sun and shade
according to our need, and read *Mrs. Dalloway*.
Can we complain? If it's our feet that hurt,

we made them so, if something else,
we have the wherewithal
as no one else to more than remonstrate.
After all, it's a window to be fed and human,
to have the sutras on our plate in translation

beside orange segments,
to walk a trail where no horde hankers
for our heads in garrotes
and we can safely sit in contemplation
without an auto-da-fé or a potato famine.

You say our ethos here is "leave no trace"?
That's bound to happen.
In heaven eternity gets touted;
in hell the lord of death holds up a mirror
and weighs our deeds in laughter.

Either way we're going someplace next,
or else it's as Larkin laments:
"Not to be here, not to be anywhere, and soon;
nothing more terrible, nothing more true."
Do you hold with this,

that death's no different whined at than withstood?
Why ruin our day in dwelling
when we might be on our merry way, not brood?
Better make our way, then,
toward the Valley of the Silent Men

where it waits beneath fraternal peaks,
that East Fork Lena byway
skirting ideation's shore
and working its way beneath walls of gneiss
past ample shares of infamy.

And through a gauntlet run of devil's club
where, abused by *Oplopanax horridus*,
we'll crowd out metaphysics,
contend instead with what those spines inject
when we're not looking.

God of wallows and greasy rock,
plaudits for this jungle throttle
we walk today, bloodied and cowed,
itching and sweating,
stung by a temporary, treatable fate

and amiably cursing, bog poisoned but irony braced:
"Thanks for leading me into this morass,
you spavined cur!" A-thrash in muck
we're snagged, rashed, spikelet daggered,
freed from Larkin's sparkless stagger,

and recalling as we trash
these large-leafed thickets
your better years so much less haggard.
"Very well!" you say. "Give me mire
and the slashing advance,

stickers, scourges, pests, jests,
of these I'll make my antidote
and sterilize those terror margins
Larkin couldn't nullify, sensate as he was—
his constant bane—to self-delusion."

But have we time for your odd therapy?
The way ahead maintains sound dictates.
And in the end we'll have to leave this river
until its rush is indistinguishable
from wind in leaves and needles

even if we're poised to listen,
even if we're patient, even if what we hear's familiar.
In other words, a stay against more staying, please,
all things being equal in a forest of return.
We've made our pact, we've chosen not to miss,

we know and knew the consequence of knowledge
and have dispensed for good with innocence.

7. WE STEP ASIDE FOR
UPHILL TRAVELERS

Tumble down this rock face, ride on scree,
rock pick, boulder hop, take it by degrees.
We'll find the line elk take conserving energy,
we'll mind time by sun's long reach
and find that time is distance,

that geography by light and not by mile
is a fine enough cartography.
They say that farther up the trail
some consequence awaits our inkling,
that one poet or another does the singing

we believe in by a high traverse,
that our stream up there is turbulent,
that the low moon in the pass
is but a step above our watershed,
that a monthlong bivouac is supernumerary

above ten thousand feet but not for penitents.
Higher still: the constellations that compose
and rearrange us day to day, each to each,
according to needs we walk with, base and stellar.
We feel a pull toward summit's reach in full retreat,

dream descending of our last pitch,
and even now discuss the crux as if indeed
it was ahead. And here's our rating system:
One a walk but two a scramble all in Arabic.
Three neglect belay at your own peril.

Four fair full of art and artifice.
Five for pitches most suspenseful.
We have our Roman long account
for summing broader scope and in preponderance.
It's relative; who can say what constitutes

a lesser or a greater route, account for seasons?
The rule of thumb is for The Brothers
when the snow is on and Constance off.
And on the trod in wind toward Crystal Pass
the chutes suggest a high aridity so many find attractive.

They say you should be goaded
by the taste of nausea,
that the northern chute is most direct—
the south easier, less likely to be icy.
"Life's a grand massif that has to be assaulted.

One chooses one's approach but on the summit
finds that weather narrows in
and then again it's to the guidebook for retreat
in dark conditions"—so pronounced your maharishi,
dwelling on his ledge as in a single or a strip.

But as for me, I'm leaving via Tunnel Creek
because I have to. I like how it goes underground,
runs fickle. I'll walk down there in search
of our refinement. Our dross is likely subterranean
enlivened, a stream incarnadine with loss—accept it.

We have to cross.
As there are rivers beyond rivers
there are mountains behind mountains.
That's cold; that takes us home.
The Tunnel Creek regress demands a ford

if it's at Monk's Camp you lay over.
You know the story—all alone, with frostbit toes,
you discover nothing there forever.
Anything described would be unconscionable;
better turn a revelation on its head

and leave it there unnoticed.
We'll have to play it such or not be given much
by sundry hikers looking for direction—
as if we really knew a thing or two
or had the signal route description.

Look, let's step aside for uphill walkers.
We'll talk their talk and keep our guard up
with politeness. For each a different silence at a read,
our palest greeting. We're hamstrung and hoary,
withered and mired. And there's the rule

that says we talk too much, that says, "Be quiet."
This might have been the problem, too, at Babel,
though on the other hand we have to be like ants
aroused by feelers. They'll tell us when to go
and when to stay, define the weather.

We've sat and talked for hours in one forest or another,
passed with but a glance of blank, mum terror.
We've been trail short and long forgotten.
We've been carried not as the acclaim that's in our heads
but as regret for what got said—

as worry over something careless misbegotten.
Awareness of us entered through a thalamus or two
and in the halls of cerebration quivered or just flashed
as light bulbs do in final incandescence—
we're just that spectral.

"Am I special?" If all of us are asking this at once
the question's moot, which might not prompt
in you redoubled pains
to make a positive impression,
to cause in travelers you pass a shock

of circuits going off and on again,
to make some bundled nerves glow brighter,
to instigate a surge or wash of serotonin:
you want to pass between transmitters
until response to you breaks forth from him or her,

another organism. Your fragile network is at stake,
your role unstable. You miss yourself
and wish you could explain it all to others:
that you were younger once and better.
You and I are overlooked at this our overlook

where we see nothing, our long-sought vista
aught and nil, not even mist that hides the mountain.
From here we view—what else?—our social status.
We're much supplanted and reduced,
we feel redacted and at the mercy of incompetence

and translation. Your center's the periphery
until we have no center, and in our public desiccation
turn to fluff and disappear in winds
of no great moment. You say that no one sees you;
you wonder at your prospects.

I would have to say what's next is pain
at every step, thoughts of rest,
and then the realizing of your trepidations—
that you will see yourself absurd and lessened,
that you will wear a gown with a gap at the back,

the better to be intubated, the better to be stented,
pricked, or trussed inside its flimsy ties and cozened.
That you are walking toward rejection.
That you will not be visited without reluctance.
That wherever there is sun

will be no home to you, abandoned.
Try me then on your water spaniels
and fly rod handles.
I'll tell you what, friend: I'll go with you.
I have a lot to do but none of it important.

Whatever happens happens to me, too;
I get that notion.
So let's wash our shirts astride this river,
dress our wounds and bathe our folds,
all those things no one else can do,

just us, with tender arms,
as such.

8. TWILIT

But you'll have to carry your own load
from one end to the other
and from here to Mount Olympus.
There we'll step onto a glacier under stars
in summer weather. We'll pass beneath the icefall

while it's cold and climb the Snow Dome.
We'll smell the sea there—salt in mountains.
We'll rendezvous for first ascents of Circe
and Aphrodite. We'll stop the sun with zinc,
take steps metered to our breath and painted.

After that we'll travel west to the Valhallas.
We won't be bothered with the possible today—
we'll walk away instead, to farther peaks,
in search of heaven and ambrosia.
And with our ancient zeal thus restored

we'll brim and wander.
We'll take our leisure rimmed with flowers
while returned to our great powers.
Where does that leave you?
Rationing the last of your figs

beside a glacier lily or an elephant's-head,
sprawled on alpine saxifrage,
plucking up the panic grass,
drying out on gravel bars,
brushing back the cattails?

Eager to turn your pack out for a breather?
Coughing up your lungs by turns,
flung against a cornice?
Doubtful we'll leave this headwall
still in concert?

Are you discontent here on our outcrop?
I hear your answer as if from a crevasse,
as if you've been entombed in rock,
as if you've joined the pontiff simonists
in Dante's bolgia. If so, you have the ears

of those two poets passing through
but for a moment. They're traveling without you,
they know the way to purgatory.
Here's a soul who lost himself,
passed beneath the gates of hell,

and lived to tell, although we know that in the telling
once again he trembled: better not to go there twice,
once on foot and once in type, as you should know,
carrying your field journal with its rain-resistant pages
and your box of sturdy pencils, recording for posterity

tangential insights and drawing sketches
of the larches as you come across them.
We have too far to go for constant comment.
This noting habit's fine for guides and mercenaries,
but for you it's a neurosis.

One further step you're in your book again,
scratching in more glyphs and syntax,
jotting down morphology as if in final edit,
as if it risked a final disappearance if you didn't.
Your many glosses are a codicil, as it materializes;

your apparatus is recyclable.
It gets thrown out, you know,
or mashed with lesser pulp or greater.
Does this mean, then, that the important thing is lunch—
a lunch always waiting in the future?

Do you want more?
If so I implore you to reconsider.

9 . BLUFF PRONOUNCEMENTS

Our way has narrowed.
We climb this hill without a purpose.
We walk as if apotheosis were at stake,
leaning against tall trees
and second-guessing. Are you familiar with it?

Our sullen forest? I don't remember
having been this way before because I haven't.
And I have lost the hang of looking at a lichen
for its own sake, though I have to add
that I have not yet given up on conks

as they are called by loggers—that fruity fungus
holds my interest for its reasonless insistence.
In fact, because it stays with trees through every season
I have been its fan through some dissension.
These clams, arboreal, are lovely, bald, tenacious.

They persist and will not go away,
like hooves or plates or shelves or shells;
they offer blunt resistance.
On high they keep stiff upper lips
above the snow line, a little comic

in their bluff pronouncement, "I exist!
And will not stop or fall because you want me to,
however incommensurate with forms of pleasure
I appear. Behold me here, a woody carbuncle
with no fear of God or you, just up here

weathering the weather minus savoir faire
or elegance whatsoever:
a blot, a stub, a nub, a butt,
an addendum,
a stubborn solitary and—did you know this?—

an attacker. One who plies the trade
of symbiosis for a while and then—a tree assassin.
And as for you, you're just a passer
with a tendency to gawk at musket balls
like me with laughter. In short,

when you're in view I give the finger.
I am the finger. Eyes forward, traveler!"
Though there are conks in certain moods
that fall to silence. Some of them are saddened
by the longer view, some private, preferring not to.

"Hard to tell what a conk thinks or feels,"
you gripe, but I see through you.
Your roving mind's afire and alights
not least upon itself from step to step,
wanders while I regale it with fungal matter.

Ganoderma applanatum doesn't pique your interest?
Just admit it; that's sufficient.

10. CROSSING THE SLIDE

Look, I'll make it up to you.
I'll walk your walk if you want me to.
I'll break trail when gloom's too much for us.
I'll shoulder our lot in life,
shoot our umbrella up instead of blaming you,

instead of praying.
I'll kick a branch from your path
with panache today—
whatever it takes, although I'm tired.
I'll stub a toe so you don't have to,

wrap your knees in gratitude,
because my altimeter reads you, my spyglass sees you.
I have a map of you—it's made of reverie.
Even as we walk I'll infer you from your gestures,
with every step I'll implore you to address me

in terms I can get next to.
Give me a sign, say you see me.
Warn me, goad me, yell into the breeze,
let me read your poems, your palm, your leaves.
I'll even listen to your litany of plant names,

or hear your lecture again on Falconiformes—
the eagle, vulture, osprey.
I'll wait while you weep for them or narrate
their stoops or hail their soaring.
I'm not adverse to you, just confused at times

by your visceral cues—though often, as we travel,
I forget about you and walk without you,
to my detriment.
I lack the training it takes
to hear you with persistence and to translate.

We could ford the Queets to Pelton Peak
and find it's still the case: my deafness.
Though it's never too late to learn a language,
never too late to navigate passes,
to account as we walk

for lateral drift and let it, without insistence.
Better still is pure dead reckoning,
though copious notes will have to be taken
and rigor applied with a mechanical pencil,
protractor, and plausible pacing.

Adjustment for the miss
should be duly factored in
before we take another step together;
I'll ask you, too, for a resection.
We'll follow the rule that governs our dominion:

beware of the trail wherever it takes you.
Getting lost a little might be beneficial,
but marooned for good, that's limiting.
Recall the more productive forms of madness—
dancing, babbling, certainty, poetry—

and there you have it, as in a slide of flailing misery,
unflagged for a crossing.
We'd have to find our trail on the other side,
the earth upended.
It wasn't in your guide—the unexpected.

Time leaves no guides except those without a reference.
What do we do, then, absent correspondence?
Certain travelers prefer the downhill runaround
and plodding scrutiny across—
fine in summer, risky otherwise,

though those who take a line
can blow it too, as can those, deploying inference,
who enter trail builders' brains,
reading hills as if they held a pick in hand
and had to wield it,

and therefore think they know which way to go
since builders choose the path of least resistance;
not so, as they are going there by dictate.
In short, no one knows,
all probe, the lacuna gets its victory,

we crown absence with our forays.
We stop on rock to think and talk.
Whipped by alder, we collaborate,
progressing mincingly, admiring fireweed—
say we avoid falling through a lattice

of downed forest,
wasn't that sufficient for our needs, by omission?
Death by disembowelment on a branch
didn't happen and it's not yet the hour for assisted living—
shouldn't we celebrate?

Maybe by this meltwater pocket redolent of snow
and stirred by chlorophyll—a damp birthplace?
We've swung around the face successfully
and found our way again but I'm not here for that,
I'm there instead as is my practice.

Am I a fool? This pool's a mirror for retraced steps
and pure enough to show me as an apparition.
So why not scoff? You have a right to.
In that case we'll sit here pointing fingers at each other;
we'll take our measure.

And when the weather changes
we'll get wet or under cover.
Okay—let's meditate by our temporary lakelet.
Are you glad to be alive today or faking it?
Always underneath each reprieve is your gloom—

could you stop doing it? For my sake?
I want to walk with you in darkness, too,
but manufacture it?
Whatever we say we'll put away
as trail's put away;

this step leaves the last one meaningless;
accretion's in your view of it.

11. THE POETS

Whatever we say we'll put away
as trail's put away:
already that's behind me
even if I elide or stet;
it can't be done again or undone

to a consummate period.
And anyway it's time to leave all talk behind
and climb steep flanks unsheltered.
We're ready for them now.
We've walked in blasts before,

and will not ask this latest rain
to stop or falter.
We've got it down our necks again
and dry our tears with it and go on walking.
We've got a stream to cross, a copse,

a bench of moonlit hemlock.
We've seen the fox up here,
the loon, the bobcat.
They're all apocryphal.
They come and go but not as we do.

They do not have our view of it—
whatever you call it
walking out or walking back,
propelled, returning.
I see myself observing every step

as if a tragedy's unfolding;
both are of my painting.
I say the words, I drive creation,
I make a downhill run
while gaining elevation.

Eve and Adam, "Hand in hand, with wandering steps
and slow, through Eden took their solitary way,"
and we do, too, and like them drop our natural tears
and wipe them soon or let them fall of their accord
upon the path that is our lot beyond the gate.

They end by walking, the world before them,
as we do on this gravel bar,
meandering down the Sol Duc.
They're freed by stain
to choose their resting place,

as are we, in scree-filled basins.
Their map's ironic:
it says the path goes where we started.
It has no legend;
its cartography feels ancient.

It can't be read by aspiration
and must be studied
late and early.
And of course they were remiss
through many generations.

They only hiked to Desolation Peak;
they didn't climb it.
They walked their high traverse instead
into a cul-de-sac of 'schrunds
and randklufts.

They blamed God for such a chilling halt
but not desire or aversion.
Whereas the walking poets
leaving hell ascended
in a winding channel

lit by shadows at the base of the inferno.
From the very bottom it led up
through alpine meadows.
They passed wan snowmelt tarns
in further reaches.

They sat to watch their fogbound disappearance.
They gleaned no essence
from the snow of cottonwoods
gathering in banks along slow waters.
They were poets on peaks, then,

monks behind temples,
never heading home or away,
never familiar, never estranged,
roaming valleys with begging bowls,
mountain lookouts, travelers, hoboes.

On they went.
Whatever was celestial for them
bore no constellations.
In paradise they recognized
the kestrel and the marten,

the salmonberries to the right of God
and owls among the angels.

At the crux we'll have to take light's measure
with neither guides nor verses.
We'll turn our childhood compasses back
and read our self-made futures.
There's an all-or-nothing pitch to our long sojourn.

There's the climber who slid
into the pink crevasse
with no last chance at sunset,
the climber who pinned the Angel of Death
in a grip that became a seizure.

We might end in limbo.
We might free-fall snow-blind
with our lives painted on our glasses.
Let's close a circle in this world, then:
there's a late slant of light to get home in.

We'll bring back freedom,
mingle in markets,
streams will meander,
flowers grow,
and love pour out of mountains.

ABOUT THE AUTHOR

DAVID GUTERSON is the author of ten books, including the novel *Snow Falling on Cedars* and the poetry collection *Songs for a Summons*. A Seattle native and a lifelong wanderer in the Olympics and Cascades, he enjoys trail and field guides, mountaineering tales, ripe salmonberries, and lolling by rivers.

ABOUT THE ILLUSTRATOR

JUSTIN GIBBENS is a Central Washington–based artist who creates images of a forgotten natural history, often blending reality and imagination. He exhibits throughout the Pacific Northwest and beyond. When not in his studio, Gibbens spends his time spotting birds and chasing after reptilian inhabitants of the shrub-steppe.

recreation · lifestyle · conservation

MOUNTAINEERS BOOKS, including its two imprints, Skipstone and Braided River, is a leading publisher of quality outdoor recreation, sustainability, and conservation titles. As a 501(c)(3) nonprofit, we are committed to supporting the environmental and educational goals of our organization by providing expert information on human-powered adventure, sustainable practices at home and on the trail, and preservation of wilderness.

Our publications are made possible through the generosity of donors, and through sales of more than 700 titles on outdoor recreation, sustainable lifestyle, and conservation. To donate, purchase books, or learn more, visit us online:

MOUNTAINEERS BOOKS

1001 SW Klickitat Way, Suite 201 • Seattle, WA 98134
800-553-4453 • mbooks@mountaineersbooks.org
www.mountaineersbooks.org

An independent nonprofit publisher since 1960